THE ROYAL COURT & THE ABBEY THEATRE PRESENT

Purple Snowflakes and Titty Wanks

by Sarah Hanly

Purple Snowflakes and Titty Wanks was first performed on the Peacock stage at the Abbey Theatre, Dublin, on Thursday 30 September 2021.

Purple Snowflakes and Titty Wanks was first performed at the Royal Court Jerwood Theatre Upstairs, London, on Tuesday 1 February 2022.

Purple Snowflakes and Titty Wanks
Written and performed by Sarah Hanly

CAST

Saoirse **Sarah Hanly**

Director **Alice Fitzgerald**
Designer **Jacob Lucy**
Lighting Designer **Elliot Griggs**
Sound Designer **Alexandra Faye Braithwaite**
Associate Designer **Anna Kelsey**
Movement Director **Rachael Nanyonjo**
Drama Therapist **Nikki Disney**
Stage Managers **Sophia Dalton, Bronagh Doherty**
Set Construction **Quiver**
Propmaking **Dylan Farrell**

For the Abbey Theatre:

Producer **Craig Flaherty**
Production Manager **Andy Keogh**
Head of Lighting **Kevin McFadden**
Head of Sound **Morgan Dunne**
Producing Assistant **Clara Purcell**

For the Royal Court:

Company Manager **Joni Carter**
Production Manager **Marius Rønning**
Lead Producer **Catherine Thornborrow**
Costume Supervisor **Katie Price**

Thanks to Dóchas Pictures for its support and charitable outreach.

Purple Snowflakes and Titty Wanks

Written and performed by Sarah Hanly

Sarah Hanly (Writer/Performer)

As writer/performer, theatre includes: **Purple Snowflakes & Titty Wanks (Abbey, Dublin/ Leicester Square/Southwark/Above the Arts/ Theatre N16).**

As writer, theatre includes: **SHOWER [part of Dear Ireland programme] (Abbey, Dublin).**

As performer, theatre includes: **One Minute (Barn, Cirencester); The Penelopiad (Jacksons Lane); London Irish Showcase (Abbey, Dublin/Tristan Bates); Moscow State Circus (Bord Gáis Energy); McDonald's 40th Anniversary (Excel London).**

Film includes: **The Hole in the Ground, Rebirth (short), There They're Their (short), Dogs of War (Shakespeare Shorts).**

Sarah was the 2019 recipient of the Pinter Commission for her new play set in Ireland during the War of Independence.

Alexandra Faye Braithwaite (Sound Designer)

Theatre includes: **Groan Ups (West End/UK Tour); Bloody Elle, Wuthering Heights, Light Falls (Royal Exchange, Manchester); Home I'm Darling (Stephen Joseph/Octagon, Bolton/ Theatre By The Lake); Neville's Island (Queen's, Hornchurch); The Audience, Juicy & Delicious (Nuffield, Southampton); Toast (The Other Palace/Lowry/Traverse); Hamlet, Talking Heads, Rudolph (Leeds Playhouse); Things of Dry Hours (Young Vic); Cougar, Dealing With Clair, The Rolling Stone (Orange Tree); A Christmas Carol (Theatr Clwyd); Romeo & Juliet (China Plate); Acceptance (Hampstead); Chicken Soup (Crucible, Sheffield); Dublin Carol (Sherman, Cardiff); Kanye the First (HighTide Festival); Room (& Theatre Royal, Stratford East), The Remains of Maisie Duggan (Abbey, Dublin); If I Was Queen (Almeida); The Tempest (Royal & Derngate, Northampton); Diary of a Madman (Gate/Traverse); Simon Slack (Soho); Happy To Help (Park); The Future (Yard); My Beautiful Black Dog (Southbank Centre); Hamlet Is Dead, No Gravity (Arcola); Remote (Theatre Royal, Plymouth); Lonely Soldiers (Arts); Grumpy Old Women III (UK tour).**

Nikki Disney (Drama Therapist)

Nikki is a state registered Drama psychotherapist, Clinical Supervisor (MA. HCPC, Badth), theatre director and yoga teacher who has worked with vulnerable groups and individuals using art for over 16 years. She has implemented and delivered Safeguarding and wellbeing procedures within arts organisations, lead on access and wellbeing for The Party Somewhere Else festival and trained artists on boundaries, trauma informed approaches and wellbeing with organisations such as Derby theatre and JMK. She has implemented tool kits for wellbeing in the rehearsal room and advised on implementing wellbeing strategies throughout institutions.

Nikki is the founder of Stage Weight Wellbeing, which focus on consultation around artist wellbeing during the rehearsal process specialising in themes of trauma, mental health and autobiographical material. Recent ACE funded R&D projects include *Aunting, Bonfires, Princess Charming, Inside Voice, Bonkers, Fandom, Summer Camp for Broken People, Enter with Boldness* and *Widows*. She has offered 1:1 therapeutic support on projects with Regent's Park Theatre,

Nottingham Playhouse and CBBC.

Alice Fitzgerald (Director)

Theatre includes: **Purple Snowflakes & Titty Wanks (Abbey, Dublin/Leicester Square/Southwark/ Above the Arts/Theatre N16); Sharp [audio play] (Bitter Pill); Bonfire [R&D] (Déda); In Vitro Veritas (Karamel Club); [scenes from] The Kitchen Sink (Edinburgh Fringe Festival).**

As assistant director, theatre includes: **Brixton Rock (The Big House); Clybourne Park (Karamel Club); Merit (Finborough).**

Dramaturgy includes: **Maiden Speech Festival (Tristan Bates).**

Elliot Griggs (Lighting Designer)

For the Royal Court: **Living Newspaper, On Bear Ridge (& National Theatre Wales), Yen (& Royal Exchange, Manchester).**

Other theatre includes: **Amélie the Musical (The Other Palace/Watermill/ West End/UK Tour); Fleabag (Soho/ Edinburgh Festival Fringe/ West End/SoHo Playhouse, NYC/Tour); The Wild Duck (Almeida); The Lover/The Collection (West End); An Octoroon (& National), The Sugar Syndrome, Low Level Panic, Sheppey, buckets (Orange Tree); Missing Julie (Theatr Clwyd); Ivan & the Dogs (Young Vic); Richard III (Headlong); Disco Pigs (West End/Irish Rep, NYC); Acceptance, Dry Powder, Diminished (Hampstead); Pomona (& Orange Tree/ National), Queens of the Coal Age, The Night Watch (Royal Exchange, Manchester); Missing People (Leeds Playhouse/Kani Public Arts, Japan); Psychodrama (Never For Ever); Blue Door (Ustinov Studio); Loot (Park/Watermill); Somnium (Sadlers Wells); Hir (Bush); Fool For Love (Found111); Lampedusa (HighTide); The Oracles (Punchdrunk); Martha, Josie & the Chinese Elvis, Educating Rita (Hull Truck); Shift, Bromance (Barely Methodical Troupe).**

Live events include: **Lost Lagoon, Height of Winter, The Single-Opticon, Alcoholic Architecture (Bompas & Parr).**

Awards include: **Off West End Award for Best Lighting Designer (Pomona).**

Anna Kelsey (Associate Designer)

As designer, theatre includes: **The Wicker Husband, Under Milk Wood, Our Town (Watermill); Microwave (Run Amok); The Sorcerers Apprentice (Southwark Playhouse); The Man Who Wanted to be a Penguin (Stuff & Nonsense); Charmane (Raised Eyebrows); Exodus (Motherlode); Guesthouse (Eastern Angles); Moby Dick the Musical (Union); Shirley Valentine (Lighthouse); The Great American Trailer Park Musical (Waterloo East); 1001 Nights (Queens, Hornchurch).**

As assistant designer, theatre includes: **The Boy in the Dress, Measure for Measure, Venice Preserved, Kunene & the King (RSC).**

Anna was Resident Assistant Designer with the Royal Shakespeare Company 2018-2019 and is a Creative Associate for the Watermill Theatre.

Jacob Lucy (Designer)

As designer, theatre includes: **The End Of History (High Hearted, St Giles-In-The- Fields); The Enchanted (Bunker); Brixton Rock (Big House).**

As co-scenographer, theatre includes: **Neverland (Parco Corsini, Italy).**

Rachael Nanyonjo
(Movement Director)

As choreographer/movement director, theatre includes: **Changing Destiny, In a Word, American Dream (Young Vic); The Death of a Black Man, Either (Hampstead); Pigeon English (Bristol School Of Acting); Cinderella (Nottingham Playhouse); Spine (UK Tour); Great Expectations (& Southwark Playhouse), After It Rains (NYT); Two Trains Running (ETT/Royal & Derngate, Northampton); Does My Bomb Look Big In This (Soho/Tara Arts); Babylon Beyond Borders (Bush); Macbeth (Orange Tree); The Jumper Factory (Young Vic/Bristol Old Vic); Misty (West End); Shebeen (& Nottingham Playhouse), Sleeping Beauty (Theatre Royal, Stratford East); Bernstein's Mass (Southbank Centre); Twilight (Gate); The Divide, Cover My Tracks (Old Vic).**

As director, theatre includes: **Recognition [audio play] (45North/Ellie Keel Productions); Bobsleigh [Old Vic Monologues] (Old Vic); An Alternative Musical [NT Learning – co-director] (National); Assata – She Who Struggles [Young Vic fresh direction] (Young Vic); 2:1 (Kanzaze Dance).**

As associate director, theatre includes: **Moonlight/ Night School (West End); Pericles [Public Acts First Stage] (National).**

As assistant director, theatre includes: **The Step Mother, Caroline Or Change (Chichester Festival); Underwater Love (Arcola/Clapham Omnibus); Kayla (Young Vic).**

As choreographer, television includes: **The Statistical Probability Of Love At First Sight, Cbeebies, Cbeebies: Christmas In Storyland, Pirates.**

As director, film includes: **Amazina.**

THE ROYAL COURT THEATRE

The Royal Court Theatre is the writers' theatre. It is a leading force in world theatre for cultivating and supporting writers – undiscovered, emerging and established.

Through the writers, the Royal Court is at the forefront of creating restless, alert, provocative theatre about now. We open our doors to the unheard voices and free thinkers that, through their writing, change our way of seeing.

Over 120,000 people visit the Royal Court in Sloane Square, London, each year and many thousands more see our work elsewhere through transfers to the West End and New York, UK and international tours, digital platforms, our residencies across London, and our site-specific work. Through all our work we strive to inspire audiences and influence future writers with radical thinking and provocative discussion.

The Royal Court's extensive development activity encompasses a diverse range of writers and artists and includes an ongoing programme of writers' attachments, readings, workshops and playwriting groups. Twenty years of the International Department's pioneering work around the world means the Royal Court has relationships with writers on every continent.

Since 1956 we have commissioned and produced hundreds of writers, from John Osborne to Jasmine Lee-Jones. Royal Court plays from every decade are now performed on stage and taught in classrooms and universities across the globe.

We're now working to the future and are committed to becoming carbon net zero and ensuring we are a just, equitable, transparent and ethical cultural space - from our anti-oppression work, to our relationship with freelancers, to credible climate pledges.

It is because of this commitment to the writer and our future that we believe there is no more important theatre in the world than the Royal Court.

Find out more at royalcourttheatre.com

 royalcourt royalcourttheatre

ROYAL COURT SUPPORTERS

The Royal Court relies on its supporters in addition to our core grant from Arts Council England and our ticket sales. 2020 was an unusual year in so many ways and we are particularly grateful to the individuals, trusts and companies who stood by us and continued to support our work during these difficult times. It is with this vital support that the Royal Court remains the writers' theatre and that we can continue to seek out, develop and nurture new voices, both on and off our stages.

Thank you to all who support the Royal Court in this way. We really can't do it without you.

PUBLIC FUNDING

CHARITABLE PARTNERS

JERWOOD ARTS

BackstageTrust

ORANGE TREE TRUST

CORPORATE SPONSORS

Aqua Financial Ltd
Cadogan
Colbert
Edwardian Hotels, London
Kirkland & Ellis International LLP
Kudos
SISTER

CORPORATE MEMBERS

Platinum
Auriens
Bloomberg Philanthropies

Gold
Weil, Gotshal & Manges (London) LLP

Silver
Left Bank Pictures
Patrizia
Sloane Stanley

TRUSTS & FOUNDATIONS

The Derrill Allatt Foundation
The Backstage Trust
Martin Bowley Charitable Trust
The City Bridge Trust
The Cleopatra Trust
Cockayne – Grants for the Arts
The Noël Coward Foundation
Cowley Charitable Foundation
The D'Oyly Carte Charitable Trust
Edgerton Foundation
The Golden Bottle Trust
Jerwood Arts
Kirsh Foundation
The London Community Foundation
Claire McIntyre's Bursary
Lady Antonia Fraser for the Pinter Commission
Rose Foundation
The Charles Skey Charitable Trust
John Thaw Foundation
The Victoria Wood Foundation

INDIVIDUAL SUPPORTERS

Artistic Director's Circle
Eric Abraham
Carolyn Bennett
Samantha & Richard Campbell-
  Breeden
Cas Donald
Jane Featherstone
Neal Gandhi & Dominique
  Mamak
Lydia & Manfred Gorvy
David & Jean Grier
Charles Holloway
Jack & Linda Keenan
The Hope Kenwright
Foundation
Orange Tree Trust
Anatol Orient
Theo & Barbara Priovolos
Hans & Julia Rausing
Matthew & Sian Westerman
Mahdi Yahya
Anonymous

Writers' Circle
Chris & Alison Cabot
Virginia Finegold
Elizabeth & Roderick Jack
Nicola Kerr
Héloïse &
  Duncan Matthews QC
Aditya & Martha Mehta
Emma O'Donoghue
Tracy Phillips
Suzanne Pirret
Andrew & Ariana Rodger
Carol Sellars
Jan & Michael Topham
Maureen & Tony Wheeler
Anonymous

Directors' Circle
Ms Sophia Arnold
Dr Kate Best
Katie Bradford
Piers Butler
Sir Trevor & Lady Chinn
Fiona Clements
Professor John Collinge
Carol Hall

Dr Timothy Hyde
Elizabeth & Roderick Jack
Mrs Joan Kingsley
Sir Paul & Lady Ruddock
Anonymous

Platinum Members
Moira Andreae
Tyler Bollier
Katie Bullivant
Anthony Burton CBE
Clive & Helena Butler
Gavin & Lesley Casey
Sarah & Philippe Chappatte
Clyde Cooper
Victoria Corcoran
Andrew & Amanda Cryer
Matthew Dean
Sarah Denning
Robyn Durie
Sally & Giles Everist
Celeste Fenichel
Emily Fletcher
The Edwin Fox Foundation
Dominic & Claire Freemantle
Beverley Gee
Nick & Julie Gould
Jill Hackel & Andrzej Zarzycki
Sam & Caroline Haubold
Madeleine Hodgkin
Kater Gordon
Soyar Hopkinson
Damien Hyland
Amanda & Chris Jennings
Ralph Kanter
Jim & Wendy Karp
David P Kaskel & Christopher
  A Teano
Peter & Maria Kellner
Mr & Mrs Pawel Kisielewski
Frances Lynn
Christopher Marek Rencki
Emma Marsh
Mrs Janet Martin
Andrew McIver
Elizabeth Miles
Barbara Minto
Sarah Muscat
Andrea & Hilary Ponti
Greg & Karen Reid
Corinne Rooney
Sally & Anthony Salz

João Saraiva e Silva
Anita Scott
Bhags Sharma
Dr Wendy Sigle
Paul & Rita Skinner
Brian Smith
Kim Taylor Smith
Mrs Caroline Thomas
The Ulrich Family
Sir Robert & Lady Wilson
Anonymous

Associates' Circle
The Board and Development
  Council of the English Stage
  Company
Drama Republic
Eric Fellner
Lee Hall & Beeban Kidron
Mark Gordon Pictures
Nicola Shindler

**With thanks to our
Friends, Silver and Gold
Supporters whose help
we greatly appreciate.**

DEVELOPMENT COUNCIL

Chris Cabot
Cas Donald
Sally Everist
Celeste Fenichel
Virginia Finegold
Anatol Orient
Andrew Rodger
Sian Westerman

**To find out more about supporting the Royal Court please get in touch
with the Development Team at support@royalcourttheatre.com, call
020 7565 5049 or visit royalcourttheatre.com/support-us**

The English Stage Company at the Royal Court is a registered charity (No. 231242)

Royal Court Theatre
Sloane Square,
London SW1W 8AS
Tel: 020 7565 5050
info@royalcourttheatre.com
www.royalcourttheatre.com

Artistic Director
Vicky Featherstone
Executive Producer
Lucy Davies

Associate Directors
Milli Bhatia*, Ola Ince*, Lucy Morrison, Hamish Pirie, Sam Pritchard (International)

General Manager
Catherine Thornborrow
Producers
Sarah Georgeson, Chris James
International Producer
Daniel Kok
Producing Co-ordinator
(maternity leave)
Tanya Follett
Producing Co-ordinator
(maternity cover)
Sharon John
Assistant to the Artistic
Director & Executive
Producer
Romina Leiva Ahearne

Head of Participation
Vishni Velada Billson
Participation Manager
Romana Flello
Participation Facilitator
Ellie Fulcher*
Participation Producer
Jasmyn Fisher-Ryner*

Literary Manager
Jane Fallowfield
Literary Associates
Ellie Horne, Nkechi Nwobani Akanwo*

Casting Director
Amy Ball
Casting Co-ordinator
Arthur Carrington

Head of Production
Marius Rønning
Production Manager
Simon Evans
Company Manager
Joni Carter^
Head of Lighting
Johnny Wilson
Deputy Head of Lighting
Matthew Harding
Lighting Technicians
Cat Roberts, Eimante Rukaite, Stephen Settle
Head of Stage
Steve Evans
Deputy Head of Stage
TJ Chappell-Meade
Stage Show Technician
Ben Carmichael
Head of Sound
David McSeveney
Deputy Head of Sound
Emily Legg
Head of Costume
Lucy Walshaw
Deputy Head of Costume
Katie Price

Finance Director
Helen Perryer
Financial Controller
Edward Hales
Finance Officer
Anais Pedron
Finance & Administration
Assistant
Annie Moohan

Head of Press & Publicity
Anoushka Warden
Press Officer
Rosie Evans-Hill

Head of Marketing & Sales
Holly Conneely
Box Office Manager
Madeline Exell
Marketing Manager (Brand
& Digital)
Joanne Stewart
Marketing Manager
(Campaigns)
Nikki Perret
Marketing Officer
Shaadi Khosravi-Rad
Box Office Sales Assistants
Tiffany Murphy*, Felix Pilgrim*, Jade Sharp

Development Director
Vicki Grace
Deputy Development
Director
Charlotte Christesen
Grants & Partnerships
Manager
Charlotte Swain
Individual Giving Manager
Amy Millward
Development Officer
Sarah Bryce

Theatre Manager
Rachel Dudley
Deputy Theatre Manager
Harvey Dhadda
Duty House Managers
Jess Andrews*, Tristan Rogers*, Sydney Stevenson*
General Maintenance
Technician
David Brown

Catering & Operations
Manager
Robert Smael
Bar & Kitchen Supervisors
Jemma Angell*, Stephen Hamilton*, Sam Kacher*, Milla Tikkanen*

Stage Door Keepers
James Graham*, Paul Lovegrove, Holly McComish*, Fiona Sagar*

Associate Company
Trybe House

Manager of Samuel French
Bookshop at the Royal Court
Theatre
Simon Ellison
Bookshop Assistant
Terry McCormack*

Thanks to all of our Ushers
and Bar & Kitchen staff.

^ The post of Company
Manager is supported by
Charles Holloway.

* Part-time.

**ENGLISH STAGE
COMPANY**

President
**Dame Joan Plowright
CBE**

Honorary Council
**Sir Richard Eyre CBE
Alan Grieve CBE
Joyce Hytner OBE
Phyllida Lloyd CBE
Martin Paisner CBE**

Council Chairman
Anthony Burton CBE
Vice Chairman
Graham Devlin CBE
Members
**Jennette Arnold OBE
Judy Daish
Noma Dumezweni
Pamela Jikiemi
Mwenya Kawesha
Emma Marsh
James Midgley
Winsome Pinnock
Andrew Rodger
Anita Scott
Lord Stewart Wood
Mahdi Yahya**

Abbey Theatre | Amharclann na Mainistreach

Located right in the heart of Dublin, the Abbey Theatre is Ireland's National Theatre. It was founded by W. B. Yeats and Lady Augusta Gregory. Since it first opened its doors in 1904 the theatre has played a vital role in the artistic, social and cultural life of Ireland.

It may be steeped in history but its year-round programme is a great mix of modern and classic plays from both Irish and international artists. There is also a wide variety of art forms, and on a given night you might also find dance, opera, music and literary performances on either of its two stages.

Inspired by the revolutionary ideals of its founders and its rich canon of Irish dramatic writing, the Abbey Theatre's mission is to imaginatively engage with all Irish society through the production of ambitious, courageous and new theatre in all its forms. The Abbey Theatre commits to lead in the telling of the whole Irish story, in English and in Irish, and affirms that it is a theatre for the entire island of Ireland and for all its people. In every endeavour, the Abbey Theatre promotes inclusiveness, diversity and equality.

The Abbey Theatre gratefully acknowledges the support of the Arts Council.

ABBEY THEATRE SUPPORTERS

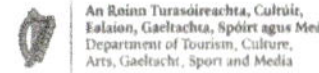

PRINCIPAL PARTNER

PROGRAMME PARTNERS

CORPORATE GUARDIANS

GOLD AMBASSADORS
Behaviour and Attitudes

SILVER AMBASSADORS
Trocadero
The Merrion Hotel

DIRECTORS' CIRCLE
Tony Ahearne
Richard and Sherril Burrows
Pat Butler
The Cielinski Family
Deirdre Finan
Donal Moore
Sheelagh O'Neill
Dr. Frances Ruane
Susan and Denis Tinsley
Lloyd Weinreb

SILVER PATRONS
Frances Britton
Tommy Gibbons
Dr. John Keane
Andrew Mackey
Eugenie Mackey
Eugene Magee
Gerard and Liv McNaughton
The Kathleen Murphy Foundation

ABBEY THEATRE STAFF

Andrea Ainsworth
Donal Ayton
Cliff Barragry
Roxzan Bowes
Aoife Brady
Maeve Brennan
Susan Bryan
Nicola Burke
Orla Burke
Simon Burke
Eoin Byrne
Maura Campbell
David Carpenter
Daire Cavanagh
Priyanka Chidgumpi
Conall Coleman
Derek Conaghy
Evan Connolly
Jeff Conway
Jen Coppinger
Fiona Cradock
Kate Crook
Richard Curwood
Mairéad Delaney
Karima Dillon
Pat Dillon
Debbie Doak
Bronagh Doherty
Colin Doran
Con Doyle
Laura Doyle
Ken Dunne
Morgan Dunne
Danny Erskine
Breege Fahy
Dylan Farrell
Eimear Farrell
Lisa Farrelly
Kate Finn
John Finnegan
Craig Flaherty
Neasa Flannery
Ellen Fleming
Robert Flynn
Veronica Foo
Tara Furlong
Sophie Furlong Tighe
Derek Garland
Donna Geraghty
Sandra Gibney
Catherine Griffin
John Gunning

Fergus Hannigan
Grace Healy
Brenda Herbert
Daniel Hickey
William Hickey
Dermot Hicks
James Hickson
Dara Hogan
Laura Honan
Narges Jahani
Vlatka Jeh
Larry Jones
Sarah Jones
Maeve Keane
Conor Kelly
Fergus Kelly
Yvonne Kelly
Ailbhe Kelly-Miller
Tom Kennedy
Shane Kenny
Andy Keogh
Phil Kingston
Michael Kyle
Luke Lamont
Marie Lawlor
Adrian Leake
Ciara Lynch
Bridget Lynskey Faust
Julia MacConville
Darren Magnier
Scott Maguire
Heather Maher
Elaine Mannion
Katie McCann
Éadaoin McCarrick
Davy McChrystal
Dan McDermott
Kevin McFadden
Róisín McGann
Aidan McGillan
Ciaran McGlynn
Terence McGoff
Grace McKiernan
Caitríona McLaughlin
Gus McNamara
Victoria Miller
Nadine-Mary Moore
Conor Mullan
Kevin Mullery
Tara Mulvihill
Aoife Murphy
Donna Murphy

Eimer Murphy
Orlagh Murphy
Agnieszka Myszka
Marykerin Naughton
Emily Ní Bhroin
Síofra Ní Chiardha
Pawel Nieworaj
Clara Purcell
Mark O'Brien
Adam O'Connell
Esther O'Connor
Colin O'Connor
Jack O'Dea
Aoife O'Neill
Tara O'Reilly
Emma-Kate O'Reilly
Selina O'Reilly
Simon O'Reilly
Valentina Quiroga
Martin Reid
Dean Reidy
Fiona Reynolds
David Roper Nolan
Josh Roxby
Pat Russell
Barbara Ryan
Aidah Sama
Joe Sanders
Andrew Smith
Sarah Smith
Fergal Styles
Cydney Thompson
Seán Treacy
Leanne Vaughey
Sean Walsh
Jesse Weaver
Sarah-Jane Williams
Sally Withnell
Monika Wlodarczyk
Bill Woodland
Damien Woods
Diarmuid Woods

BOARD

Mairéad Delaney
Peter Lowry
Máire O'Higgins
Michael Owens
Dr. Frances Ruane (Chair)
Michael West

Purple Snowflakes and Titty Wanks

Sarah Hanly is a writer, actress and owner of the production company Dóchas Pictures. As writer, theatre includes: *Shower* (as part of *Dear Ireland*, Abbey Theatre, Dublin). As performer, theatre includes: *One Minute* (Barn, Cirencester); *The Penelopiad* (Jacksons Lane); London Irish Showcase (Abbey, Dublin/Tristan Bates); Moscow State Circus (Bord Gáis Energy); McDonald's 40th Anniversary (Excel London). Film includes: *The Hole in the Ground*, *Rebirth* (short), *There They're Their* (short), *Dogs of War* (Shakespeare Shorts). Sarah was the 2019 recipient of the Pinter Commission for her new play set in Ireland during the War of Independence. Sarah is currently working on commissions for theatre and television. Dóchas Pictures will produce television, film and theatre projects.

SARAH HANLY

Purple Snowflakes and Titty Wanks

and

Shower

faber

First published in 2021
by Faber and Faber Limited
74–77 Great Russell Street
London WC1B 3DA

Typeset by Brighton Gray
Printed and bound in the UK by CPI Group (Ltd), Croydon CR0 4YY

All rights reserved
© Sarah Hanly, 2021

Sarah Hanly is hereby identified as author
of this work in accordance with Section 77 of the
Copyright, Designs and Patents Act 1988

All rights whatsoever in this work, amateur or professional,
are strictly reserved. Applications for permission for any use
whatsoever including performance rights must be made in
advance, prior to any such proposed use,
to Casarotto Ramsay & Associates, 3rd Floor, 7 Savoy Court, Strand,
London WC2R 0EX, *tel* 020 7287 4450

No performance may be given unless a licence
has first been obtained

This book is sold subject to the condition that it shall not,
by way of trade or otherwise, be lent, resold, hired out
or otherwise circulated without the publisher's prior consent
in any form of binding or cover other than that in which
it is published and without a similar condition including
this condition being imposed on the subsequent purchaser

A CIP record for this book
is available from the British Library

978–0–571–35744–4

2 4 6 8 10 9 7 5 3 1

Contents

Acknowledgements

Many thanks to the generosity of people who gave up their time to come to readings, read drafts, offer rehearsal spaces; as a student coming out of drama school, it was these people who believed in the work – who helped to make it happen. Lots of people I would like to thank are in the production pages. With deep reverence to the Christian Faith.

Vicky Featherstone, Mel Kenyon, Alice Fitzgerald, Jane Fallowfield, Catherine Thornborrow, Lucy Davies, Sharon John and everyone at the Royal Court Theatre. Jen Coppinger, Craig Flaherty, Neil Murray, Caitríona McLaughlin and all at the Abbey Theatre. Alexandra Faye Braithwaite, Rachael Nanyonjo, Elliot Griggs, Jacob Lucy, Nikki Disney, Sophia Dalton, Bronagh Doherty and all our team. Jodi Gray, Nick de Somogyi and Dinah Wood at Faber & Faber. Leo Butler and all in the Royal Court writers' group. Sherrill Gow, Jacqui Somerville, Christina Kapadocha and Mountview Academy of Theatre Arts. Peter James CBE and the Old Diorama Arts Centre. Beat Eating Disorder Charity. Lexi Clare, Emma Hall and John Brant. Peter and Anthony. Imogen Sarre. Goril, Yvonne, Christine, Carolyn, Denise, Bernardo, Jaz, Maddie and Debris. Mum and Dad. Peter Hanly and Catherine Hanly.

PURPLE SNOWFLAKES AND TITTY WANKS

For women gone before
Coming behind and those here by my side,

for my Sisters everywhere.

Purple Snowflakes and Titty Wanks was first performed in a co-production at the Abbey Theatre, Dublin, on 30 September 2021, and at the Royal Court Jerwood Theatre Upstairs, London, on 1 February 2022. The cast and creative team was as follows.

Saoirse Sarah Hanly

Director Alice Fitzgerald
Designer Jacob Lucy
Lighting Designer Elliot Griggs
Sound Designer Alexandra Faye Braithwaite
Associate Designer Anna Kelsey
Movement Director Rachael Nanyonjo
Drama Therapist Nikki Disney
Stage Managers Sophia Dalton, Bronagh Doherty
Set Construction Quiver
Propmaking Dylan Farrell

For the Abbey Theatre:
Producer Craig Flaherty
Production Manager Andy Keogh
Head of Lighting Kevin McFadden
Head of Sound Morgan Dunne
Producing Assistant Clara Purcell

For the Royal Court:
Company Manager Joni Carter
Production Manager Marius Rønning
Lead Producer Catherine Thornborrow
Costume Supervisor Katie Price

Characters

Saoirse

in the world of the play

Giant
Pilot
Ashling
Orla
Father Mick
Daisy
Sister Patricia
Mrs O'Heffer
Bishop Pádraig
Aoife Kelly
Mrs Toad
Beth
Anna
Maria
Glitzy Principal
Brenda
Jacinta
Otillie
Brendan
Gabriella

Neighbour, Cónal Flynn, Mr Glynn, Reverend Mother,
Psychoanalyst, Police Officer, Nurse, Hospital Chaplain,
Pope Joan

Note

Saoirse plays herself and other characters too.

Pilot can be pre-recorded by Saoirse or another actress.
Giant can be pre-recorded by an actor.

A (/) indicates an interruption of speech.
Mini pauses are indicated by (–) which can indicate a
change of rhythm, thought or character.

The pace is set by the space given between lines.

Saoirse has the agency in the storytelling. Any props that
Saoirse needs, she can get from a bum bag.

External objects which enter the space can be a beanstalk
(green rope), a cake, a confetti cannon and the natural
growth of the earth; flowers, crystalised stones and feathers.

The set is bare and can become covered in the debris of
mess. The edges of the set can reflect different levels of
height, depth and width. All of which can aid a flight
witnessed in Saoirse's mind. Her proprioception can become
more and more distorted, quieted, numb; moments of
stillness can invite us in to all,
that comes from nothing.

Through light, sound and the physical decaying
of what is on display, we reach spiritual,

Clarity.

All can be made
new through the fog;
a sense of luminary transcendence.

Though, now –
We begin,
in a voided pit.
Painfully, present.

Too bright –
Frozen in time.
Forgotten in space.

Longing to remember

–

Like a fire longing to be sparked,
Lowly burning,
Like a beetle waiting,
yearning – to remind of all
that can spring
from earthly presence.
Awareness,
Stillness.
Nothing . . .

*The play went to press during rehearsals and may differ
from its presentation in performance.*

A FLIGHT

Plane door opens. Light shines out.

Saoirse Hello?

Pilot Flight to Dublin.

Saoirse and company,
    this is your final call.

Sound of a flight taking off.

Giant We're expecting turbulence;

Giant Máis é do thoile;

Pilot Please.

Giant Éist liom;

Pilot Listen,

Giant Go cúramach;

Pilot Carefully.

Darkness.

Ashling Overly horny?

Saoirse You ask, you seem intrigued.

Yes, I says.

Ashling In what way?

Saoirse You says.

I don't know, I'm just veryvery horny.

I don't know how else to put it.

Ashling Right.

Okay.

Are you having the sex?

Saoirse You ask.

God no! I says, I've never had sex, Ashling but while you were out, I've learnt how to make my own orgasms.

Ashling What's an orgasm?

Saoirse Um, I don't really know how to describe it properly. But it's this feeling that just shoots through your body like an electric current.

Ashling How in God's name do you make that happen?

Saoirse Practice and determination. I says.

I can show you if ye like but you're not to tell anyone I do it okay?

Ashling nods.

Okay.
    Right, okay.

    *Saoirse takes anal beads out and uses them to aid the
    storytelling.*

I use these.

Ashling You put them, inside you?

Saoirse No-way I says. I tried them up my bum once and I
tell ya,
    It was some operation getting them out again.

Orla taught me first, it happened by chance!
    We were giving each other tickles in the oratory –
    The holiest room in St Maria's Enniskerry.
    And we were going quite high up on the thigh, just
beside my –

Orla Do you mind if I tickle here?

Saoirse Orla says.

Nono I says. I don't mind, do you mind?

Orla Nono!

Saoirse She says.
    Course we didn't fuckin mind.
    And it was really actually more the getting to the place
before actually, getting there – the journey to the.
    Yes Orla! I like that –
    Oh, hello!
    Guess we could try it back there too,
    I've never – but Orla has
    and she says it was like.

A grenade explosion.

Someone needs to explain this,
    like verbally, and maybe –
    demonstrate, with a fake . . .

Bumhole?
Is that okay to say –
Anal sex okay let's call it, it's an anus.
Weird name for a word,
sounds like (*Pronounced like 'Shame us'.*) Séamus –

And then Orla just tickles her beads over the top of my vagina and this sensation just rippled through me whole body like a wave of fire!

And you're going to want to keep rubbing, at this point, to keep the feeling going as long as you can.

Ashling Shush Saoirse,

Saoirse You says,

Ashling The nuns will hear you.

Saoirse They're well used to us by now, I says, we're having them like three or four times a day. We're inundated asking to go to the toilet and I tell ye –

They know we're not going for the shits and giggles.

Ashling Gosh Saoirse. Have they ever seen you?

Saoirse No way Ash, though they could probably do with having a feckin look themselves!

You can borrow the beads if you like?

Saoirse My father left a few years ago, he just fucking vanished so we held a fake funeral for him. But the truth was, we hadn't a clue where he went.
     And it'd be a sin to live in a house without a paternal law so,
     we tell the neighbours:

'Very sudden. Big shock, ye. Well, yeno –
     gradual decline and then.
     Boom. He departed' –

Neighbour Sorry is he dead or alive?

Saoirse A neighbour says.

Oh ye, think so.

Father Mick You're either one or the other, death is finite –

Saoirse Father Mick says, friend of the family.

And our Mum's been living with him ever since.

Ashling Your mum lives with a priest?

Saoirse You says. Yeye Ashling, I says, say nothing to no one because it would cause,
     Holy feckin war. Wouldn't it?

It fucking would.

Would it?

So, me and my sister, Daisy hold the fort. She's been going mad because the shower was blocked again! Our toilet in Enniskerry had a tiny little hole and I was forever blocking the loo with a shit tonne of toilet paper, I needed it to drown

out the splashing sound my vomit would make. And the
shower was also clogged with cornflakes, pubes and hair so,
  I had to move onto plastic bags after that.
  And I meant to flush them down the loo before Daisy –

Daisy Two Dunnes Stores bags, full of puke!
  Ugh, why the feck are these under the stairs? You'll be
sorry in a minute.
  Don't fuck with me Saoirse. What will become of your
talents if you keep doing this?

Don't answer the question, it's for you to think about.

And secondly,
  Tell me two life goals, right now.

Saoirse Eh I want to play a real woman in the school play
and,
  then emigrate. I says.

Daisy You are not,
  going anywhere till you've done the leaving cert.

Saoirse Daisy tries to talk like a 'Dublin 4' Ash to fit in
with her posh mates and she says I talk like a Howiye –
  Neither of us belong anywhere.
  And she's out the back garden there
  chucking the puke onto the flower bed.

Daisy It's compost!

A tiny stalk emerges from the flower bed.

Saoirse She says.

Ashling You make yourself sick Saoirse?

Saoirse You says.

Ashling That's not funny.

Saoirse Ye I know Ash, I says but it numbs the pain in my
head and I like feeling empty after.

Ashling You really shouldn't do that Saoirse.

Saoirse You says.
  Ye I know I says –

Ashling I mean it Saoirse –

Saoirse Yeye okay Ashling!
  I hear you. But you should eat.

Something.
  I says.

Saoirse 'We made a deal here,' he says.

Sister Patricia You made a deal where?

Saoirse Sister Patricia says.
    Yeno the sub-teacher
    who we bring wild stories too!
    Think she likes the talk; pretends she doesn't
    but she always sits, wide-eyed and still.
    And we, are the queen time-wasters,
    so –

Nono Sister, I says.
    Cónal Flynn says, 'we made a deal here, if I made you
cum, you'd suck my dick,'
    eh sorry Sister –
    his willy,
    whaddya call it,
    penis.

His penis Sister!

Sister Patricia Oh, I prefer willy.

Saoirse She says.

Sister Patricia It's a little less,
    I don't know,
    on the tongue.

Saoirse Exactly Sister, now you're with me –

Sister Patricia Nono,
    I'm not going there with you.

We're going back to the biology book, if you want to
know about that;
    I don't know,

Ask your mother.

Saoirse She lives with a priest.

Sister Patricia Oh! Really?

Saoirse Let me show you Sister, if you don't mind – I want
to,
    help you
    help me,
    understand because Cónal
    pushes my head down and I sucked it for a while.

    Saoirse gives a blowjob; this lasts for quite a while.

And I didn't really know what I was supposed to be doing
and eventually he gets annoyed at me and asks me to give
him a dick massage instead.

    Saoirse gives a very bad handjob.

I didn't really know how to do that either so he gives me a
hand.

    *Saoirse gives an enthused handjob whilst trying to look
    pretty. Saoirse whispers to him –*

Come on.

    Saoirse finishes.

We got there eventually Sister, I was over the feckin moon
when he finally ejaculated all over himself. And she's
watched the
    whole performance Ashling and only now,
    she says;

Sister Patricia Saoirse, I have a duty now to, to ask you,
    to leave.

A moment. Sister Patricia is enjoying this; she reclines in her chair.

Saoirse No problem I says. But sister;
  I puked on his penis and I had to suck it *all* back up and swallow it because, I was afraid of him seeing.

He was a clean freak. and I knew he'd kill me if he saw it and after he was like –

'Aw babe, that head wasn't the worst actually. It was so wet.'

Ye, I bet it fucking was.

Ashling Saoirse Murphy!

Saoirse You says.

Bear with me Ashling,
  And she's closed her eyes.

Are you saying a prayer for me Sister Patricia?

If you're still in there Sister, it's because I have a bad gag reflex from, overusing the muscle for another activity, so I guess my question is,

how do you pleasure a man without knowing how to?

Or if you want to?

Or.

How not to prematurely climax and then
  lose the deal,

or
  just teach us to say
  No!

There it is –
  Women are conditioned to do what they're told –
  We are not

Taught
how to say:

No.

You're really flushed, will I open the window, red face.
    Like a red apple; Yes!
    It's about the apple and the garden and whose sin
became who because that's what it all boils down to.

We need to re-address the apple sinner too.

    The stalk glows.

Sister Patricia We do not! She is fine as she is.

Saoirse But if she is made to be a big evil whore,
    or a virgin,
    or a perfect mother –
    and if that's all she can be,
    well then she becomes a –
    well a.

An immovable object;

    The stalk grows a bit.

And I fucking move around Sister.

    The stalk grows a bit more.

And I need you to meet me here –

    The stalk has one more growth spurt.

And before I know where I am.

I'm kicked out the door.

Saoirse So I end up in front of the principal.

I'd like the right,
    to renegotiate my punishment.

    *Mrs O'Heffer calls Mrs Murphy. She speaks into an
    office phone and uses the dangly wire to fiddle with. Mrs
    O'Heffer picks moments with the wire to be twizzled,
    extended, or she can wrap herself in it in moments of
    distress. Mrs O'Heffer speaks lowly, with a thick, rural,
    Irish accent. Mrs O'Heffer holds tension in her fingers
    and her lips are pursed. Saoirse can hear Mrs Murphy's
    responses; distantly and high-pitched.*

Hallo there is that Mrs Murphy?

Ah how are you Brenda? Listen; It's Máire O'Heffer from
St Maria's Enniskerry.

I'm not too bad thanks Brenda, how are you?
    Very good.
    Now, wait till I tell you.
    I have Saoirse here in the office and she's actually been
speaking sexu-ally

explicitly.

Devil tongue – Ya. Ya. Ya.

It's nine forty-five a.m. we haven't even done the rosary yet.

Mmm

Mmhhmm.

You know, I think there could be some mental problems there, I mean she's sixteen and she's talking about cunnilingus!

Mrs O'Heffer tries to say this in private; she covers her mouth.

No it's oral sex I believe.

Ya.
    Ya.
    Great stuff.
    And we just can't handle her any more and she's disrupting the learning of the other pupils. So!

We are taking her out of classes and putting her into one on her own and a drama club she can exert her, talents, there! Ya.
    Okay so Brenda we'll see you at the school show.
    And how's Father Mick?

Very good. Okay.
    All the best.

God bless.
    Bye.
    Bye now.
    Bye bye.
    Bye Brenda.
    Bye bbb bbbyyee bye God bless bye bye bye Bye bye bye bye

Bye now.
    Bye bye bye bye bye
    Bye bye Brenda
    The Lord loves you!
    Bye
    Bye!

Mrs O'Heffer hangs up. Saoirse puts the phone back in her bum bag.

Mrs O'Heffer Six weeks' detention with, no trips to the
toilet,
    in any class.

Saoirse She says.

Mrs O'Heffer Or, you play the King,
    in the school play.
    And you commit your life
    to the stage,
    the only place
    for your,
    clowning.

You do whatever you like
    with rest of your time,
    and then find your way,
    into the male roles,
    you are too much woman

for a,

well,
    for you.

Saoirse Ugh I wanted to be Antigone I says,
    because she has everything taken from her
    and she is like all the lead women I read about
    and I want to play a real woman and
    she is the most real thing I get to
    existing, in this
    place, Mrs O'Heffer can I at least be Ismene –

Mrs O'Heffer Saoirse, this is not
    an open debate –

Saoirse Fine, I says.
    I'll take the man.
    And I leave.

Brief white noise – tinnitus.

Saoirse makes a loop round to a toilet cubicle.

And I down my pasta in one.
    And I head off to the loo and I.
    Projectile the shame out of me –

The thing about pasta is,
    it flies straight back up in one go.

I avoid carbs when I'm trying to be skinny so when I'm
bingeing I have a bit of a carbohydrate party.

Oh and chocolate, I fucking love chocolate, the thing about
chocolate is it tastes just as good coming back up as it does
going down so I get to experience it twice.

I have to be careful with cornflakes though because if I
don't let them dissolve in my tummy for long enough they
scratch my oesophagus on the way back up.

I hate letting them sit there for too long though because I'm
afraid of the calories absorbing into my blood so I put up
with the pain.

Well actually I kind of like the pain; is that weird?

Oh and bread is also an awful pain in the arse to bring back
up, if I don't chew it properly it comes back up in lumps
and I do be heaving over the toilet for ages.

Sometimes I just eat and spit, chew, spit. Chew, spit.

Bread is a terrible one for creating a splash in the toilet too
– if I'm not careful I get a load of sick in my eye –

Fucking nightmare.

Saoirse walks out of the cubicle.

And I walk out and you're in, Ashling!
    You're never in –

And you –

Ashling fixes her uniform in the mirror.

And your hair's fallen out but your eyes are
	Very bright –

You look well.

I says.

Ashling is displeased.

Ashling Were you being sick?

Saoirse You says.
	Nono I says. I haven't done that for ages –
	And I eat a nibble of the tiniest piece of pasta,
	left on the lid of my lunchbox.
	And you leave for practice –

And I couldn't believe it I'd never seen you in the gear
before.
	And I watch you doing laps of the hockey pitch.
	Your legs are covered in this downy hair.
	Mine are too.
	And I spit the tiny pasta bit I'd been sucking
	and slip it in my pocket.

And the bodies in these uniforms feel
	so restricted –

Saoirse moves to try and sit with the bodily discomfort.

Saoirse One More Tune! Deco's Disco!

Jarring music plays: 'Poker Face' by Lady Gaga.
Saoirse does a high kick and starts Irish dancing from left to right. Saoirse's body is rigid and her dancing is to the beat of the music. Saoirse's face is deadpan. Music cuts.

We were like two horny devils, running from Deco's disco into the church car park that night. Honest to fuck Ashling, I didn't really know what I was getting meself into.

After Jack O'Quiffe finishes aggressively fingering my vagina, which was rather painful to be honest.

I'd never had anything up there before.

I didn't even know if I had a hole.

Well I tell ya; we made one after this.

He straightens up and says:

'Right I'm going to make this simple, give me a titty wank.'

A titty wank? I says.

'Yes.'

He says.

'Give my cock a wank with your tits.'

I nearly fucking died I was a thirty-two double-A I'd no tits to wank him with.

So he takes his trousers down and I pull my top up and shove my two fried eggs together,

Burger nips they used to call me

My nipples were bigger than the actual tit

And he whips out this chode of a thing

And starts trying to rub it up and down

In between my tits.

Saoirse demonstrates, whilst trying to look pretty.

But there's nothing there so he's just grinding on my sternum! And let me remind you, we're in a fucking church car park and all.

I'm going to hell for that if nothing else.
    People are passing by so he turns me around to block his cock.
    'Quick Saoirse hide my willy there goes the Bishop.'

Saoirse turns to hide and waves to Bishop Pádraig.

Evening Your Grace!

Saoirse squirts hand sanitiser all over her face and chest.

It doesn't take him very long before I'm covered in his manly juices.
    Now what do I do?
    I says.
    Father Mick is dropping me home!
    'I don't know,' he says, 'sort yourself out.
    I'm heading back in to the lads.'
    You can't fucking leave me here I say, in a church car park covered in cum. 'See you later ye, got to run.'

–

Don't worry Ashling it's only hand sanitiser.

Giant Can you wear a sexier bra.

Saoirse examines and rubs down her stomach as Giant echoes.

Titty wank.

Saoirse tit-wank!

Get your tits out get your tits out get your tits out for the lads,

For the lads!

Tit-wank Murphy.

She's a bit hairy for a blonde.

Gave good wank –

Not enough tit, Cónal got head off her.

Was she tight?

Fuckin didn't get the ride did ye Jack.

Saoirse Mr Glynn's been teaching us how to put the
numbers in the ledgers Ashling;

'Close your legs girls my eyes are wandering.'

Aoife Kelly Why are you looking up our skirts sir?

Saoirse Aoife Kelly says, so she gets taken out of class.
     And then a few days later he's allowed back in
     and she is moved to a different class . . .

Is that what actually happened?

Do you remember that Ash?

He did it a lot. 'Put your jumpers on girls your shirts are
see-through.'

So few months later, I stand opposite my sister, Daisy, in the
dress rehearsal of the school play;

And I'm wearing fake balls,

> *Saoirse takes fake balls in tights out from her bum bag.
> Saoirse zips them into her bum bag so they hang low,
> between her legs.*

I take this *really* seriously.

Something empowering about this
     I don't know what but
     I like using the bellow and
     taking up this much space; this is more fecking fun than I
thought it'd be.

Mrs Toad Saoirse. Tone it down a bit –

Saoirse Mrs Toad says, so I give it even more;

(*Overly RP.*) You there!

Mrs Toad Just, 'you there'.

Saoirse (*overly RP*) You there!

Antigone's after burying her brother –

'You there,
    studying the ground,
    hold up your head and tell us, is this true?'

And by the time of the performance
    in front of the entire school
    I realise,
    this is fucking brilliant –
    I am commanding the stage here.

    Saoirse walks with wide strides; balls swinging.

And I never want to come out of this role.
    It's like a drug,

it makes me feel alive Ashling.

And I'm in the wings.
    And I hear the pupils taking their seats.
    And I know my mum and Father Mick are somewhere in
the audience.
    The adrenalin flooded in Daisy; playing Antigone.
    But me,
    I'm as cool as a cucumber because
    I think everyone will only look at her as she's playing the
broken-ish woman in a pretty dress and then I realise,
    this is the most real I've ever felt, playing Creon,
    thank you Sophocles.

And just before the house lights go down it hits me
    This is just a part.
    So it's never going to be enough.

And I say a quick Hail Mary.
    And I'm thinking about

being able to walk about so freely, chin high
head higher –
chest open, stance wide,
not feel like a prisoner
in a ship never shown
how to use its own –
but sailing freely,
and what that might be like
here in Enniskerry –
To hold the gaze of a male

and be the last to look away.

The lights come up –
and I can't stop imagining my life in another way.

So I'm saying the lines but I'm thinking of
What lays beneath,
tired; wrongly conditioned to fit a
Gaze for only one
when here, we are fucking two –
so I

I relish in the moment of:

'You there!

Did you or did you not know that the proclamation
forbade all this?'

And Mrs Toad is sighing
And in walks titty wank,
and I notice Sister Patricia here –
and Mr Glynn too.

So, I grab my balls and

*Saoirse grabs her balls out from bum bag and holds them
high.*

I hold them high, and Daisy is just staring at me.

'Do you have any idea what you have done to our women?'

And no one has a clue I've gone off script –

Saoirse rests the balls around her shoulders. They hang either side of her chest.

but Daisy's laid down,
    pretending to be a corpse.

'You must trust your intuition girls, before they teach you
    to forget.'

And the girls are screaming!

Father Mick over here, I says –
    he's as reverent as they come.
    And he, has a secret wife!
    You heard me.

And Mr Glynn at the back's a perv.
    And Aoife Kelly was made the villain.
    Which she of course accepted!
    Because we are deeply conditioned.

And Sister Patricia is mouthing.

Sister Patricia pleas with her right palm to the side of her mouth; to aid a painfully loud, voiceless:

Sister Patricia Staaaand doooowwwn!

Saoirse And Jack at the back –
    made me wank his cock.
    And the Sister here,

Daisy Leave me out of this.

Saoirse Not you Dais –
    Blessed Patricia,
    who I asked to show us how.
    Denied my request so,
    I was left with –
    Cum on my chest.
    And I would like to know,

Saoirse takes the balls off her shoulders and gathers them up tight.

as the King here,
	because apparently that gives me

Saoirse beats the rhythm out of:

basic human rights!

The balls bang into her open palm.
	The stalk grows.

What will the compensation *be*
	for the business ledger that.

Mr Glynn, has made me forget how to do,
	Because my body is triggered by the sight
	the sound the touch the taste of
	His sin –
	And I've ignited Daisy.
	She is up from the dead.
	Fire in her eyes –

Daisy And I, have
	polycystic ovaries.

And I want to know why I haven't been taught about more roles for women in the history books! Because surely they were fuckin around –

The stalk grows.

Saoirse And I fucking second that!
	In the kingdom on earth that,
	is here for us to view
	if you taught us in the classroom
	so we wouldn't have to rub them out
	in the loo /

Ashling Saoirse Murphy, I still can't believe you did that on our school stage.

Saoirse Yeye Ash.

It was feckin different every night.

In another life, no.

I got expelled.

Ashling Ye and they never let you back in Saoirse.

Saoirse Ye I know,
    I says and you were out too.

A PURPLE?

Saoirse You remember my final day at school,

I came in to collect all my stuff.

We thought it was so normal, to just not go.

Or did we?

Anyway, Orla's lurking
    in the lockers.
    Our relationship was one of those;
    Fluid ones.

Orla loved the tickles as well.
    Mind you I was still only attracted to women by this
point –
    I just hadn't a feckin clue!

Orla Quick up to the holy room, you up for it?

Saoirse Orla says,

Up for what?

I says.

Orla Let's scissor each other's legs before you go –

Saoirse She says.
    Oh right, why not! I says.
    And so we go up to the holy space,
    And she's a shoulder of vodka for me
    As a leaving present . . .
    And I down some.
    And we hoist our skirts up.
    And the morning prayers start ringing –

Church bells chime loudly. Saoirse fights the urge to climax too soon –

So I am.

Saoirse is close to climaxing as choral music plays over the top of the bells.

Hail my
    Queen –
    I give you
    My,
    my.
    Just
    on the cusp of,

Saoirse's orgasm begins as Sister Patricia enters. Saoirse sees Sister Patricia; Saoirse jolts down and works hard to conceal the hormonal rush.

and in walks Sister Patricia
    As Orla says,

Orla Stick your finger

in my,

ass
    hole,

gently;
    if you're up for that! Nownow –

Saoirse Oh.

And so I collapse on top of Orla.
    –
    Are you
    o-kay? I says –

Have you an underlying heart condition or something Orla?

Orla Nono I just love your legs.

Saoirse She says.
  Of course you do.
  I says
  oh God,
  that explains it,
  You were very, receptive as I was
  resuscitating
  you –
  I thought,

is she really unconscious
  But, you were –

Oh hello Sister!

Sister Patricia Saoirse Murphy!

Saoirse She says.

Sister Patricia Do you think I am some duck?

You have been banned from the property.

Saoirse It was a complex procedure Sister –
  Stepping out.
  I thought,
  I'll go up to
  the holy room
  and mark the moment.

and who do I meet
  On her deathbed, Orla!

And the leak above,
  Saturated Orla's –
  And the only thing
  The only thing Sister,
  that brought her back to life –
  The drip,
  And, also –
  my kiss,

combined.
–

And then, well you walked in
So you know,
and we don't name the floods Sister,
we follow the instinct of the drip.
Satiating in the, feckin nip.

And she's out the door like a shot.
    And then she comes charging back in with Mrs
O'Heffer –

Mrs O'Heffer Saoirse,
    Sister Patricia
    informed me
    on what
    she walked in on.
    And I should tell you –
    They have a view
    of those sorts of
    preferences.
    I know you're
    leaving but
    Orla, if you're staying,

Be aware who you
    talk to.
    Or –
    Do. That –
    Not on our premises.

And I leave.
    The look on her face when I collected the results –
straight A's.

Mrs O'Heffer I don't know *how* you did it,

Saoirse She says.
    And an award for English and drama.
    I worked my hole off in the confines of my bedroom!

Mrs O'Heffer Saoirse, by the way, you can't be a lesbian –
and I'll tell you why –
   Lesbians don't have blonde hair. Mrs Foley our hockey
teacher is one and she has, a different way, which is more,
discreet,

Than you.

Saoirse –
   No wonder I wanted to emigrate after that.

The shame made me ill.

Ashling Saoirse are you a lesbian?

Saoirse You says.

I don't know I says I like vaginas, they're nicer lookin and
more compact.

I fucking hate the word lesbian. I wish it had a different
name.

Ashling Like what.

Saoirse You says. Eh.
   Like purple I says.

Ashling Purple!

Saoirse You says. Yeye I says – your favourite colour –
   I'm a purple, that's nicer,
   I'm going to call myself a
   purple Ashling.

Giant Your teacher's on the ball. No purples allowed in
Enniskerry!
   Where'll the tit wanks come from?
   Oi oi!

THE SUGARLOAF MOUNTAIN

Saoirse sits on top of a mountain's edge. Wind blows strongly.

Saoirse By the end of summer, it had been two months since I last made myself sick.

Ashling I'm so proud of you.

Saoirse You says.

And it was the first time you'd worn your new wig out in public. Do you remember, I curled it for you and we made it look really nice.

And your sister dropped us to the Sugarloaf mountain, she told me that you had a granola bar in your bag and she'd love if you ate it.

So I stop off at the corner shop and buy a box of Celebrations to make you feel comfortable.

Did you notice I did that?

And halfway up the mountain your feckin flip-flop falls off –

Would you have worn better shoes woman.

And I give you a piggy-back up and we reach the top, but the wind, it nearly takes the skin
　　that's left off your face.

　　Saoirse and Ashling sit down on top of the mountain.

Do you remember that Ashling?

Ashling Ye I was four stone.

　　Saoirse's feet dangle over the edge.

Saoirse So I'm digging into my Celebrations to make you feel at ease.

And you actually took out the granola bar, I couldn't believe it because I'd never seen you eat Ashling. I barely looked at you but I was giving you the sneaky side eye and digging into the Malteser flavours.

Saoirse takes out a Malteser wrapper from her bum bag.

Is that why you ate the bar?

A long moment.

Saoirse looks out at the view; where the Earth's edge meets the clouds in the sky.

And we sit in silence for a bit, I didn't want to make a thing of it.

The wind blows very gently now. Saoirse holds Ashling's hand; resting on the ground beside her. Saoirse tickles Ashling's fingers and then squeezes her hand again. It is a gentle, firm hold. Saoirse leans her head in and their heads rest together. The wind is even gentler now; it kisses Saoirse's skin – barely touching at all. A magical moment of natural beauty is engulfed on the mountain's edge, as the view becomes still and the world is all a quiet dream below; stillness, frozen memories in time; the girls sit and take it all in.

I'm so proud of you! I says.

Ashling I'm going to get better

Saoirse You says.
And a little while later –

You take your top off –

You showed me what you'd done.

You showed me that you'd carved a crucifix into your chest.

*Saoirse takes a red lipstick from her bum bag. She carves
a crucifix into her chest.*

I never said this to you but that really affected me.

And I didn't really know how to deal with the situation so,

Saoirse stands up.

I walk away and –

I wish I had more patience with you.

And you follow me –

Ashling Here, have this gift.

Saoirse Kilkenny crystal.
And you tell me all the reasons I deserve
all this love –
for all the healing,
I'm doing –
why my life is worth living.

And I felt so helpless because it was –

You who needed.

We both did.

And I am out of options so –

I need to tell you something – I says.

I'm moving to Musical Theatre School in England at the
end of the summer.

Ashling Why do you need to go away?

Saoirse You says.

Ashling Just stay here – or I could come.

Saoirse And it's making me sad
because you're sad.
Don't cry – I says.

I just need to go.

And you leave –

   Saoirse watches Ashling walk down the mountain.
   Saoirse calls after Ashling.

You can't walk home I says, not from here.

It'll take you hours Ashling –

Ashling I need to burn off the calories.

Saoirse You says. Just stop for a minute
   I says. Please.
   And I tell you –
   If Aoife Kelly could get better
   then so can you Ashling –

Ashling Aoife's anorexia wasn't as bad as mine –

Saoirse You says.
   That's not the point, I says –
   she was going deaf and blind and now
   she's recovered,
   and you don't back down so
   I let it go –

And I wish I knew the right thing to say.

And then we stopped for a while,

I regret ending like that –

Do you remember that Ashling?

   Pause.

That was around the time you went back into hospital and
they started force-feeding you.
   I know you hated them sticking the tubes in you but I
was so relieved because it was the only thing keeping you
alive.

So then I head off to Musical Theatre School in England –
    You really didn't want me to go.

Ashling Saoirse Murphy.

Saoirse You says.

Ashling I don't think Musical Theatre School will be good
for your eating disorder.

Saoirse Well I can tell you something Ashling Daly.

You were so feckin right.

And I left and I started this new life in England. And I never
told anyone about anything.

And I was fine –

Essex.

Beth Are you alright babe?

Saoirse They says. Am I alright? I says.

Anna Yes babe. You okay?

Saoirse An Essex person's way of saying how are you. Conas atá tú Ashling, ye I'm fine, why, do I look sad? And then I almost feel sad cuz they're asking!

Are *you* alright? I says.

Maria Ye babe!

Saoirse England.
    And the girls are chanting.

Sounds of the girls chanting, faintly:

Anna If you want to be a dancer you've got to trim your thighs,

The sounded musical rhythm of the beat plays.

If you want to be a dancer you've got to trim your thighs.

Saoirse That's just the body dysmorphia, I tell them.
    Your thighs are absolutely fine.

Maria Nono.

Saoirse They says,

Maria The weigh-in lady after ballet says it.

Saoirse And they're all measuring each other's waists with tapes and eating lettuce.

I, on the other hand, am still playing men. And so I'm
writing an email to the head because I'm sick of it –

Glitzy Principal You'll have a big part end of year, trust me.

She says.

And will I play a real woman?
    I says.

Giant An underfed sex bomb going mad.
    Needs a shag.
    Victim eyes.
    Naughty gal.
    Perfection.

Saoirse –
    I tell her I need to make it here –
    Please.
    I can't go back.
    And I need you to let me play the brokenest most
    distraught woman
    so they can see
    I can –

Glitzy Principal Broken woman?

She says –

Glitzy Principal You'll be playing the strongest woman love
– this is your training.

And I don't fucking understand because I am in the balls
again,
    And I was going for Juno not Jack the Paycock!

And I'm stood in rehearsals, hair tucked under my cap.
    And a handsome suit and
    I have a massive crush on my friend Maria.
    She's playing my wife
    and I,
    I realise what it might be like.

God I'd be so much kinder than they were back home.

Cinematic music underscores.

'The whole worl's in a terrible state o' chassis,' he says. And he's right! Thank you O'Casey.

Beth 'Chassis', are these Irish musicals.

Saoirse Nono, *plays.*
I says. and we also learn how to play consent, for roles, in shows –

Ashling They teach you consent?

Saoirse You says, ye Ash –
They should teach this in real life.
it's like a choreographed movement,
I touch your right cheek with my left hand –
And then I move my left foot towards you.
Put your hand down my thigh,
That's fine ye – I'm okay with that.
And every movement is carefully constructed,

Can you believe it?

One blossoms blooms on the stalk; a passion flower.

Thank you Jesus!

An enormous cake drops in a cake box.

Skype calls.

Fuuucckk!

Saoirse puts two candles in: '8' and '3'.
She lights them and sings.

And it's your birthday Ash, I know I'm a day late –
They didn't have twenty,

so I put in eighty-three.

Saoirse sings.

Lá breithlá shona duit.
    Lá breithlá shona duit.
    Lá breithlá shona duit.

Happy twentieth birthday!

Blow from Ireland.

    A moment.

C'mon ya granny –
    make a wish.

–

    Well my wish is to remember the female body,
    at every age, and stage,
    because I think they should be made holy.

    Saoirse blows the candles out.

Will I go to hell for saying that? Joke.

Oh feck I might. Sorrysorry.

No I'm, not feckin sorry.

I've been in hell, this,

this is what hell is,

What's your wish Ashling?
    –

    Saoirse tries to offer a slice through Skype.
        Billie Eilish's '8' plays. Saoirse stares at the cake.
    Blackout.

    Saoirse stares at the cake.
        Blackout.

    Saoirse stares at the cake.

I'm not doing it. I'm not doing it.
    Blackout.

Saoirse crouches over and inhales from a protective hold.

Blackout.

Saoirse stands right back.

Please God.

Blackout.

Saoirse eats the cake, manically.

Blackout.

Saoirse throws the cake at the walls.

Blackout.

Saoirse crouches against the wall, disassociated, numb.

Blackout.

Saoirse struggles with the cake, she manically dances around it.

I'm not doing it I'm not doing it.

Daisy I'm giving it a go at the Sisters of Mercy –

Saoirse Daisy says.

Daisy I can't have children so I might as well,
   give it to God.

Saoirse Fair fucks to ye!
   I says. And so, I fly home.
   And next thing I know, we're sat in this hall.
   I've had three gin and tonics
   and Daisy's wearing a lovely suit.

(*To Daisy.*) You're a fucking ride.
   I says.
   And the new sisters are being welcomed
   and the head of the pack gets up.

Reverend Mother Most promising sister in training,
   for her work in inner-city Dublin and indeed,
   with the elderly, here in our own district, goes to –

Daisy Murphy.

Saoirse And she's up
   giving a speech.

Daisy Gosh –
   I wasn't expecting this.
   Okay –

*Daisy has come fully equipped for the award. She takes
out a pink microphone.*

How are ye.
Good,

Thank you!

Saoirse She thinks she's won the feckin Oscars Ashling,

Daisy I would like us to be in suits, not the dresses it's the twenty-first century and they just feel a bit century. We're advancing with the times and I urge you to empower us.
    That's my blessing to manifest, for this prize –
    Put us in suits. Okay lads.
    Good luck ladies.

Saoirse puts the mic back in her bum bag. Saoirse claps manically, cheering.

Saoirse Fucking excellent.
Well done Daisy. She's my sister!
    And I'm off my tits so I'm escorted out to the loo
    by Father Mick.
    Bear in mind it's a very quiet occasion.
    Not many were invited but because of his,
    Perks of the patriarch – the holy fam
    Made it in.

Daisy and I head into town after with an older woman.
    Jacinta!

Saoirse frenetically signposts the journey.

And we leg it through the halls,
    past my mum and Father Mick!
    And I plant a big kiss on Sister J.

Brenda Oh Saoirse, not here love.

Saoirse Mum says.

But the whole formality sort of makes it,
    impossible not to.

These institutions are minted Ashling,
    the amount of people making donations –

hoping to save their souls when their souls are feckin
fine –
somebody should tell them!

Saoirse grabs Daisy's microphone out of her bum bag.
Saoirse cowers and secretly bellows, deeply into the mic.

The souls of women are intact, women own their own souls.
And Father Mick is making his way back over to tell me;

Father Mick The two of you made a holy show of us.

Saoirse And he takes his secret wife home.
And Daisy and I,
ended up at some after-party, and I have a threesome
with –
Hello Jacinta. And a man with crocodile eyes!
Jacinta, I says.

Are you allowed to do this kind of thing?

Jacinta I've not been initiated, yet – and you Saoirse, well
You could turn me!

Saoirse Turn you from?
Oh. Daisy's a bit perplexed,

Daisy Saoirse are you gay?

Jacinta O'Reilly said you, took her to places she's never
been before.

Saoirse Did she?

Daisy Ye, can you not see I want to have a real go at this
Saoirse.

Saoirse Yeye no problem, I says.
And I've been calling myself a *Purple* here –
Because sometimes I just don't want to define it at all –
do you remember that Ashling?
Or did we ever talk about that?

And I'm feeling manic from the comedown,
    so I decide to tell my mother *all* about it.
    –

    And then I
    I just licked it –
    Mum.

Sorry what would you say Mum?
    Went down on her?

Eh, lick-out.

I licked her out Mum.

I personally find them too tickly.
    So I give them.

Brenda Oh right.
    Very good Saoirse, I did that with Michelle Cooke for
years!
    Only joking!
    Do you have
    friends you can do this with –
    We won't
    Talk like this in public spaces.

Saoirse She says.
    Why not, I says, the boys do.

Giant Your mum understands.

KINK!

Saoirse So, I'm back in England and I have BDSM with
Otillie –

Ashling Her name is Otillie?

Saoirse Yes Ashling it means prosperous in battle, she told
me while we were fucking.

Otillie Bondage Sadomasochism!

Saoirse She says.

They did it for years in the brothers, flagellating, it can be
quite an act of –
    Kink!

What are these for?
    I ask her, as she strokes
    her canes and whips and chains!

Sound of Otillie playing with her toys. The sound builds.

Otillie To tie you from the ceiling.

Saoirse She says,
    oh right – I says.
    Very good!

I nearly feckin died!

I'm a bit nervous,
    she's older than me,
    a graduate.
    She was helping me settle
    in Ashling!

Ashling I'm sure she was.

54

Saoirse You says.
    And she's giving me a tour of her flat.
    And her hand is on my lower back.

So we start with the fridge.
    The coolest water
    in bottles from Ocado, with
    pink flowers on the front.

And the ice cream is
    Freezing and twenty pounds!
    Minty, vegan.

And the snacks are
    Spicy and the pizza is
    Extra doughy but gluten-free!

And before we know where we are,
    A living-room floor has never felt more appealing.
    This is like nothing
    I've ever experienced!

Till she says:

Otillie I had a dream you slept with my neighbour.

Saoirse Oh right, I says –
    What the fuck were you dreaming about us for.

Ashling Sounds like she's trying to be kinky.

Saoirse You says.

Ashling I read about that once.

Saoirse Oh, okay.
    I fucked your neighbour I says okay I'll play.
    Now what?
    And before we know where we are –
    She's ordering four hundred pounds' worth of new toys.
    And I order a takeaway.

Both arrive on express delivery!

And I shouldn't have eaten so much because now
    I can't stay present.
    And the body, here –
    Which, if it wasn't such a place of shame.
    Might actually be enjoyed.

So I'm thinking about how much.
    I've consumed.
    And random lines from.
    Juno.
    And the Paycock.
    Are floating through my.
    Periphery.
    And I forget
    to call the
    safe word.

So she's giving me a good,
    hiding and I, am –

Remembering. The
    woooooord.

Ah,
    and that was the problem,
    there is too much forgotten
    to be present;
    So I
    Ah
    stop stop stop,
    Mother of mercy!
    Sorry.
    ow,

    –

    I was thinking about
    Ah! Ow! Nono no biting.
    Oh okay,

ye –

And the pain makes me feel alive, like I'm here.

Like I'm present –

I fucking love it.

That was actually quite nice Ashling.

Giant Ye this is fucking great, can I play?

Saoirse Piss off!

Petals falls away from the stalk. A storm brews.

Music plays in a club. Lights distort a very present reality. Saoirse stands on an edge. All becomes a blur. Saoirse releases into a back-bend. Sound and lights cut to a pier at night. The light of the moon and stars cast spells upon the gently roaring sea below. Saoirse is really present in a chaotic state; she takes her ringing phone out of her bum bag. Saoirse answers a call.

Saoirse Hello Mum, it's Saoirse Murphy.

Oh you rang me.

What are you up to?
  –

  Yeye I know,
  I got the WhatsApp.

In a club, ye.
  Came out to.

–

I don't want.
  I don't what to talk.

Yeah.
  When?
  She did,
  yeah.

–

I tried.
  Went twice before and.
  Tried again, do you know what?
  –

Oh.

Yeah I don't want to.
    Can you make an arrangement.
    –
    I don't know.
    No, because I'm at the pier.
    Southend Pier ye.
    The water looks nicer in the dark.
    It's black, it's so nice.

What? Nono I'm not doing that any more Mum!
    I got the help book you sent me it was really helpful.

Red wine.
    –
    One glass.
    We also need to talk about Daisy.
    I didn't think she was able to have babies.
    Can she keep training in her.
    Girl gang, wolf pack,
    Whaddya call it
    Feckin. Sisterhood?

Ugh.

Dicks.

    –

I don't know if I'm coming.
    Can you just drop it.
    –

Please for the love of God
    just listen to me,
    For fuck sake.
    –
    Sorry
    Yeye. I will okay.
    –
    Love you too.
    Bye.

Saoirse And I'm in the Christmas holidays of my final year at Musical Theatre School.

My hands don't feel like they belong to my body but other than that,

I'm doing fine,

so I'm at this party I hadn't had anything to drink I was just.

Exhausted Ashling!
    And I needed smokes so,
    I crept out,
    drove the car thirty seconds down the road.
    I drive into the theatre school car park;
    the building looked massive in the dark
    so I thought,
    maybe I'll go in.
    And I can't see too well.

I go round the bend.
    And I just keep turning and turning.

Sure didn't I park in the reception of the theatre school.

Car crashes loudly into a building. Sounds of the windshield and glass on the front of the building, shatters. Saoirse takes it all in, her bonnet is ablaze and the car has three wheels.

A moment.

Fuck.

Saoirse sees the receptionist. Saoirse rolls down the car window; the sound of the squeaky window plays.

How are ya!

I'm sat there, digesting the fact that,
    I've given Flo, the receptionist, a heart attack.
    Sheer terror, Ashling.
    Sorry about this Flo, let me reverse –
    So I do.
    And I drive through town with three wheels and a
blazing bonnet.
    So I am sent to see this man, psychoanalyst.

Saoirse sits down and takes him in.

He wears a kilt.
    Hello, I says.

A few seconds.

He doesn't speak, His technique is, wait for you to speak.

A long moment.

You are infur-iat-ing, I says.

A longer moment.

Fine, I'll play. I have a dead heart. One-third of it died when
I saw a bird choke in the door of a cage, two-thirds of it
died when I knocked my fanny bone against the corner of a
desk, worst pain and the final third died when I ate salt and
vinegar Taytos and the kids told me they cause hearts to die,
    we were influenced in all sorts of ways! and so, my
garden has endured many years of man-made pain, to
emerge from a bulimic hell pit and be touched again, by
nature, silver lining! And I give the rest of me away to
strangers, mostly women and children.

Psychoanalyst Are you in active bulimia?

Saoirse He says. Gosh no! I says. I'm just living.

–

Analyse me then,

–

just fucking fix me,

A moment.

you're wasting my session.

A longer moment.

Fine, you won't speak! I'll be you!

'Saoirse, you only ever think about yourself, you're never sincere because you don't know what it is to be truthful and most shamefully, you're a bulimic who can't control herself.'

That's not nice!

I says.

'You play other people because you have no idea who you really are. Your body is a constant reminder you are not worthy to live in it because you don't take yourself seriously so nobody else does too. You've no friends, a broken family and you puke and puke and puke which wastes everyone's time because you just projectile everything everyone gives you, back in their face, like the evil fucking villain you are. And you'd love to be with anyone, but you can barely sit with yourself, so you'll die alone and rot in hell.'

Saoirse takes a moment.

Jesus.

Saoirse focuses back on the psychoanalyst.

Who lets you practise?

Psychoanalyst I would never say that.

Saoirse He says. And then I say, playing myself:

So I love to leave you and I leave to love you. And all I really want is connection, paradoxically. I am too fucking terrified of letting anyone near me, touch me see how broken I really am. I eat food and throw it back up to feel anything, other than me; Shame reeks bloody mercy. I live a pointless, fractious existence. Life is so fucking unfair.
  Was that good?

Psychoanalyst (*pronouncing her name wrong*) Saoirse. Is that how I say it?

–

Saoirse He says.
  No. I says.

Psychoanalyst We've reached the fifty-minute mark.

  Saoirse checks the time.

Saoirse It's actually two minutes to –

Psychoanalyst So, how much can you pay?

Saoirse And we fight over the extortionate fee – and I end up kicked out the door!

Saoirse makes her way across the back, to a small toilet cubicle.

Saoirse I'm doing the kids' panto in a library in Dagenham.

We carry the set in a feckin van Ashling!

Saoirse takes out a large bag of white powder from her bum bag.

And eh, ye. It's great. But you'll never guess what I did.

We were snorting lines in the loo and I took too many. I've never tried this before –

How do you open the bean bag.

Saoirse tugs the bag.

So I give it a good tug.

Saoirse showers herself with white powder.

And lo and behold.
Snowflakes all over the place.
Worse, it was all over our costumes.

So there we were like feckin eejits –

Saoirse tries to pick up the powder from the ground.

Sniffing it off each other's legs and arms –

(*Pronounced how it's spelt.*) shcooping it off the floor.

Beanstalk (green rope) drops. Saoirse moves towards it. Saoirse hits her head on an iron gate.

Ow!
    Where did the iron gate come from?

A child in the audience shouts as Saoirse makes her way to the rope –

'Mummy what's Jack doing?'

The child's mummy responds.

'He's not well poppet, Jack is, sick.'

And the parents leave and I'm –

Saoirse speaks rapidly as she mounts the rope.

So I walk up to the giant's castle and I –
    Leap down the stalk –

Saoirse slides down a bit.

Hereyehereye!

Saoirse outstretches her torso and waves one arm, manically.

Oh yes I did.
    Sorry wrong bit.
    Oh no it's not.
    Oh yes it's not.

Saoirse slides down the beanstalk rope and sits to the left of it.

Where are you all going.
    My brain is tired Jack,
    the car needs petrol and what happens,
    if you don't know where your car is.
    So I lay there for a while
    making angels in the snow.
    Where is everyone going,
    I'm having a party – Feckin pricks.
    Santa's NOT REAL!

Ashling Saoirse.

Saoirse Sorry Ash.
   I –

Ashling Line your stomach.

Saoirse You says.

Ashling Just go home –

Saoirse Home?
   I says.
   It's too late –

   *Saoirse takes another line. She swivels round to the right
   of the rope; she looks up and sees the face of a Police
   Officer crouched down, looking over her. Saoirse's
   proprioception is really off balance. She gets too close to
   his face and quickly backs away.*

Wow, you look like St. Patrick he banished the snakes the
fuckin legend,
   And you know what Brigid did?

Policer Officer No?

Saoirse Me neither. The police officer's looking over me –

   Saoirse tries to become a bit more sober.

Policer Officer Have you taken any drugs darlin?

Saoirse He says.
   No. I says.

Policer Officer Do you take drugs?

Saoirse No!

   The Police Officer pulls Saoirse up.

Policer Officer We need to take you to hospital to look at
the drugs in your system.

Saoirse Calpol,

*She tries various different ways to hold herself upright
and stabilise herself.*

Codeine, horse tranquillisers, paracetamol,
    that sort of thing.

*Saoirse has moments of real tension with the Police
Officer, she allows for stillness before falling on top of
him.*

Where are my trousers?
    I mean I'd believe it ye, oh! And he says –

Police Officer We'll do a blood test.

Saoirse Cocaine and tequila.
    And Calpol, I fuckin love that one.
    The pink one like I –

*Saoirse falls off-balance and holds his hand – as she
manages to keep herself upright, leaning on him.*

Do you have any?

*Saoirse skips around the space and really enjoys this
moment of getting into the ambulance. Lights and sound
puncture Saoirse's fragmented and chaotic travel.*

Don't look at me like this!
    I forget what I've come from and that's the whole point,
    earth suit is a ball ache and the emphasis –
    Officer, is on the ball.
    It's gas Ashling.
    We're all here in the back of the nee-naw –
    I won awards Officer
    and I used to be really good at this –
    I just forgot how to.
    Came before,
    Heart wasn't
    connecting, to – glorify in the,
    the.

Giant echoes.

Giant Can she do the tit wank again or else just
        face the wall and give us a break?
        Face the wall and give us a break.
        Face the wall and give us a break.

Nurse You can't be trying to take your own life,

Saoirse The nurse says. I didn't? And I'm trying to see clearly but the room is spinning.

And the chaplain has been called in and he's standing over my bed

like I've a pot of gold beneath me –

(*To Nurse.*) Do you do BBQ spare ribs here? Wow you kind of look like Fred Astaire.

He's a tap-dancer, you just reminded me of him there the way you moved the tray.

Hospital Chaplain We were giving you the last rites Saoirse.

Saoirse He says, oh right I says.

I've always wanted those.

And then,

she arrives, Mum!

Followed by Daisy.

And around the corner,

My own father walks in Ashling!

   Saoirse sees him enter. Long pause.

Dad.

Brendan Saoirse what have you gotten yourself into now?

Saoirse He says.

Brendan I've been living with monks near Rome. I love them as much as I love you, so –

I did it for all of us.

Saoirse Daisy can you get me Doritos, I says.

And Dad's getting emotional –

Brendan Saoir saoir,

Are you okay?

Saoirse You know Dad that's a trick question over here.

Brendan You're not doing the puking thing any more are you?

Saoirse Nono Dad of course not.

Brendan Great, and well my only friend, Father Mick. Who I know lives with your mother. He was the only one to have known about my walk with,

the monks.

And he sent me a voice note on WhatsApp to say you'd hit your head on a gate in a library in Dagenham and from the wind through the blower, you were hooked up here the next day, weren't you?

Saoirse Ye.

Brendan Great.

Brenda Saoirse.

Saoirse Mum says.

Brenda If we are going to be paying your school fees.

You, you.

You can't be doing

co-caine.

Saoirse Gosh Mum would ye stop, it was only a one-off.

Brendan Brendan. No Saoirse, that is a class A drug.

Saoirse I like your hair Brendan, did you get it cut? It's lovely, you look like the Pope.

Brendan Oh, well.

Thank-you very much.

On that note.

I forgive you –

Saoirse And here comes Daisy.

She's brought Doritos Ashling,

Excellent and this is awkward, Dad's crying.

Brendan Are you having a baby or did you eat your way over?

Saoirse She met a fisherman in São Paulo Ashling and now she's pregnant.

Brendan Saoirse, is this because I left for the monks?

Saoirse Well, it was a bit traumatic but like,

you're here,

oh my God he's about to overshare –

Brendan I live with monks, near Rome –

Saoirse We heard you the first time,

Brendan So,

We all feel a bit, responsible do we, for Saoirse being,

the way she is,

Saoirse Rude!

Nurse Oh no,

Saoirse The nurse says,

Nurse We use the three C's here, we didn't cause anyone's disease we can't control anyone's disease and we can't cure anyone's disease.

Saoirse I don't believe that I have a disease; I says.

I am dis-eased by this situation, yes, and the only thing I have to control my voided existence is a blanket of chaos.

It keeps me alive. To take it off would be, too real.

You ran away to join a closet Brendan –

why do you judge mine!

And I don't need anyone to tell me how I should, or shouldn't play roles,

or how I should or shouldn't internalise all the homophobia but what if I didn't want to call myself a purple or can I not be a lesbian because I have blonde hair . . .

Who made that rule?

Giant I made that rule it's a bloody good rule.

Saoirse And I am so fed up of this giant fucking voice, hardwired in my head so that a world based on balls-only constructs, led by *just men*, can remain enforcing rules, on the body, basic human rights, but who's to say that some people in this world aren't worthy of piety or connection to something greater, than this.

We all live here!

It's one of the biggest atrocities known to humankind.
    And yet calling it –
    Naming it; well that opens up shit for them,
    and everyone would love to avoid facing their realities
because well.
    Need I say feckin more –
    It's a holy show!

We never knew all of this, did we Ashling?

But this here,

it's like I'm living,
    but I'm dead,
    I am shot to pieces and I carry on . . .

Brendan Saoirse!

Saoirse Dad says,

Brendan You sound pro-found.

And I know I, I know I taught you how

to read and –

Daisy Brendan, I I wouldn't –

Saoirse Daisy says,

Daisy The point I think she's trying to make, correct me if I'm wrong Saoirse, women need to step into their own, step up to an equal playing field –

Giant Which woman are you being now?

A fuckable virgin,

a sex-driven, hungry sinner,

or a hormonal mother?

Saoirse Fuck off. And I am used to making everything into a fairytale because this is the only way to make sense of the –

Chaos, too much to go into for a hangover,

can you knock me out?

Do you do that here?

And I've downed the Doritos and I

don't do what I normally do I, just take it all in.

Brendan I'm so sorry love,

Saoirse Brendan says,

Brendan It was, the shame;

I guess we wear it as a nation, so

I needed to get away –

I'm so

So

proud of you Saoirse.

Saoirse Thanks lads. Thank you.

POTATOES!

Saoirse So I'm back in Ireland for Christmas Ashling. And Daisy's about to give birth.

Brendan Were there many at my fake funeral,

Saoirse Dad says.

Brendan Come on, tell me who went and, who didn't. Oh I'd love to have been a fly on the wall –

Saoirse And Father Mick and the Bishop are all round the table,

for the modern family dinner.

Brendan Father P is now a bishop.

Saoirse Dad says.

Brendan So don't talk about,

the hijinks in Dagenham.

Saoirse He's seen my tits Dad,

so I think we're past that!

Brendan Excuse me?

Saoirse Yeah yeah, sounds good Brendan!

Daisy My own are lactating.

Saoirse Daisy says.

Daisy Mind you I don't miss shoving Tampax up once a month but I know my anus might rip from the birth and I'm okay with that –

Saoirse She says.

And Ashling, it was the best moment of my life.

You might poo too, so feckin what like.

You're birthing a human, women are fucking

Amazing.

So Father Mick's gone green here.

And Mum's bringing the starters –

I don't know about you Ashling, but

I've always dreaded the Christmas holidays.

And all the different types of food . . . the potatoes alone:

Saoirse examines the potatoes spread across the top of the table. She analyses each dish speedily.

Mashed potato
   Boiled potato
   Rosemary roasted potato
   Potato wedges
   Jacket potato
   Potato salad
   Sweet potato
   French fries
   Leak and potato gratin!

Nothing compares to the guilt I felt when I stood up to go to the toilet after the dinner.

Daisy Saoirse, Mum's turkey was eighty euro and for you to puke it all back up, you selfish fucking cunt.

Sorry, hormones!

Saoirse So up to the toilet I go.
   Puke it all back up.

Saoirse loops quickly round, running back to the table. She runs another circuit around the space.

And then straight back down for round two. This was on a
loop Ashling!
    I was out of control. Meringues
Strawberry cheesecake Chocolate cheesecake Pavlova
FRUIT CAKE
Honeycomb ice cream Vanilla ice cream Chocolate fudge
brownies Chocolate biscuit cake FERRERO ROCHER.

*Confetti cannon bursts with sound. Gold confetti rains
from above.*

Ashling Did you keep the dessert down?

Saoirse You says.

The look in my sister's soft sad eyes.

*Saoirse plays her sister.
    She stands still for a long moment.*

Daisy Please.

*Saoirse struggles to attempt another loop. Sounded
rumbling; turbulence.*

Saoirse But even that couldn't stop the urge to purge.

*Saoirse arrives on her knees after being sick. Saoirse
zones out; stillness. Brief white noise – tinnitus.*

So I went up to my bedroom and puked in a Dunnes Stores
bag even though I knew it had been too long and the
calories would have definitely absorbed into my blood by
now.

So.
    To get rid of any extras.
    I mix some Epsom salts in water.
    Down them in one.
    Fucking rotten they are.
    And wait for them to kick in.
    And for the explosions out me arse to start.

Brief sounded intestinal explosions.

But just to be sure.
　　To be sure to be sure. To be *sure*.

Upbeat Christmas track plays: 'It's the Most Wonderful Time of the Year' by Andy Williams. Saoirse begins an exercise circuit. She varies between star-jumps, bleep-test runs, tuck-jumps, sit-ups and bicycle obliques. This descends into a manic, frenzied struggle until she collapses flat on the ground. Giant laughs.

Giant Your teeth may erode, not bad thing given their length.

Twelve pubs lads, where's tit wank she's home for the holidays.

Any wanks?

Saoirse So I'm back at college Ashling and I'm making myself sick around, twelve times a day.

Think I've eroded my oesophagus away now cuz I get sick without even sticking my fingers down my throat.

I'm completely dead and gone inside now.

I feel like my soul has left my body and I'm just floating through life somewhere.

And when people try to speak to me they're just speaking to my remains.

It's really weird.

I don't know if this makes sense Ashling.

My mind is fucked these days. Like foggy. Yeno?

This started just after you died actually.

Ashling I died?

Saoirse You says.

Ye.

But I pretended in my head that you didn't and we carried on having our conversations.

Do you remember the last time I visited you?

I felt sick with nerves walking down the long, sterile corridors.

And I remember the ceilings were really high, like so high and there were palm trees just dotted around everywhere . . .

I walked into your room. And there you were.
   I barely recognised you.

And I felt so guilty.

Because you said you remembered we were best friends.

And then you says:

But something happened.

I can't really remember, you says.

But we stopped being close.

And I started to feel really bad for.

Yeno.

Not being there.

And pushing you away after the whole crucifix thing.

We chatted for a while and I told you all about Musical Theatre School and you told me all about your organ failure.

And I don't know why but I just couldn't believe you. We hugged and kissed and said our goodbyes.

   Saoirse hugs Ashling.

And you were so delicate so I held you gently. And I left.
   And a little while later I'm back in England and I get a WhatsApp from Aoife Kelly.
   Ashling Daly died.
   I remember the shock.
   You couldn't have died Ashling.
   You were going to live.

And my best friends from Musical Theatre School were all holding me. Maria, Anna and Beth.
   All holding me and stroking my head.

Maria I'm so sorry Saoirse.

Anna I'm so sorry.

Saoirse They kept saying.
    And I fell onto the bar in the night club in Southend; and I couldn't even cry for a while.

I wasn't really present after that.
    I wasn't really present for a long time after that.

A high-energy, remixed version of 'Country Roads' by John Denver pulses.
    Saoirse stands still for the duration of the song. This should be jarring. Illuminous yellow sunflowers grow throughout.

I'M SORRY

Saoirse I went home the next day for your funeral.

And I watched you being lowered into the ground.

Ashling Daly.

Written on your gravestone.

Died.

Aged twenty. I'm still twenty.

You says.

I'll always be twenty.

—

Do you remember those stories I used to tell you to make you excited about living? The stories about:

Fighting with Sister Patricia.

And playing Creon in the school play.

And BDSM with Otillie –

Did I ever tell you them?

I keep replaying them over and over in my head; I'm just trying to pinpoint where I lost you, and then you says . . .

Saoirse desperately searches for the words but can't find them.

Well I don't know what you would say . . .

I'm sorry I wasn't there for you. I'm sorry I wasn't there to help you eat more granola bars. I'm sorry I didn't know the right things to say.

I'm sorry I left you behind,

CLARITY . . .

Saoirse cleanses herself with water and washes away the debris. Saoirse becomes aware of her breath and her body. Saoirse puts a clean top on. Incense and light lead Saoirse into a spiritual awakening.

Saoirse's paths begin to renew as she transcends through ritual, to a place of grounded, earthed being. Music is tranquil and divine. Clear light shines in the sanctified space.

Present.
  Whole.

Awoken.
  Awake.

Anew –

Pink cherry blossoms bloom.

Saoirse So I step into my best role yet, it's the final show.

Daisy Have you got the balls on?

Saoirse Daisy says,

No, I've hung them up –

I says.

Because I'm playing Pope Joan.

Giant I took her out of the history books –

Saoirse I know, that's why we're doing the play! And I was so fucking angry to be playing a woman who has to pretend to be a man to take up space and then I realised.

That's what I've been doing!

And I thought I had to play the broken, beautiful, women seen only through the giant gaze viewed by the whole fucking world.

And I'm slowly realising, I don't.

But the thing is deeply intrinsically flawed . . .

So I end up writing an email to my principal – she's actually written the main part for me and I'm complaining, how am I ever going to get signed if I'm looking like this – I need to wear . . .

Giant The sexy bra?

Saoirse Ye. No, I mean.

I just want to be a woman playing a woman for once in my life!

Giant The crazy woman?

Saoirse No.

Giant The perfect wife?

Saoirse Fuck off.

And my family are here in the foyer –

Brendan What? A woman pope?

Saoirse Yes, Brendan, Pope Leo made her cardinal and when he died, she was elected pope and when she was found out to be a woman – stoned to death.

Giant Good.

Brendan Oh, I read about this.

Saoirse Dad says, yeye I says, she gave birth during a papal procession!

Brenda Good woman!

Saoirse Mam says –

Giant I changed her name.

Saoirse She was documented till they made her a myth! And ever since Mam, they have a testicle chair, designed like a loo, with a little hole, for the genitalia to be checked.

If you have balls you're a pope – and if you've ovaries, you're not.

Daisy Don't ruin the play.

Saoirse Daisy says, I won't I says. I'm just letting you know, it all comes down to, the testicles! Beth plays the ball checker for the pope elected after I die. If I hear her say the line one more feckin time – 'Testicoli che ha e quelli ben appesi'

Meaning: testicles he has, and well-hung ones!

Giant You're making me uncomfortable / can you –

Saoirse Great! And then it hits me.

I realise this,

this is the part; most interesting.

Giant Don't get too cocky.

Saoirse And Daisy's popped her tit out and she's breast feeding here in the foyer.

Daisy I hope this is suitable for kids.

Saoirse She says. She's brought her fisherman hubby, Pablo, and my niece and god-daughter, Gabriella,

she's a little angel.

And this

is the business Ashling.

I'm about to do it.

 Pope Joan gives a blessing in Latin.

Pope Joan Lupus pilum sed non vitium perdit.

Saoirse Meaning the wolf sheds his pelt but not his characteristically vicious behaviour.

And in the audience,

I remember the face of the

creepy business teacher

and the biology sister

and titty wank –

And I throw my grad robe off,

and we take the final bow –

Step step, centre and, hold.

Right hand up to the gods and hold two three four,

tits and teeth six seven,

and bevel, smile, don't wobble –

Bow!

Stagiest moment of our feckin lives Ash.

Saoirse leaves through stage door. The voice of Giant becomes warped and unclear.

Giant You have great stage presence Saoirse. We'll nurture you darling.

Saoirse steps up and out. She walks a newly lit path.

Saoirse And I realise as the lights comes down.
She was the realest woman I've ever played.

Saoirse sits in a garden shed with clear glass windows. She watches a robin land in a bed of twelve white star gazer lilies. And twelve more passion flowers. Saoirse looks over an outdoor pit filled with feathers and crystalised stones.

Saoirse I eventually step out of roles and come back to Ireland to take a look.

Mum, Dad and Father Mick are all heading off to Rome, maybe they're just openly reforming the church!

Polyamorous lads?

Brendan No Saoirse,

Saoirse The weather's better over is it. I see the benefits!

And I start to do really well, and I make my offer for the family home; paid for it, outright, that,

is my final offer – I says.

And I turn it into a sisterhood.

A freedom dream.
    Saoirse Aisling.
    Spelt the way it means,
    but sounding like, planting your spirit, here too.
    There's an outdoor pit, just for feathers, crystals and
    Salt stones! A gal pad, Ash,
    This is where we rest.

We practise stepping into big roles
    like Taoiseach
    President, Cardinal and we also,
    teach consent.

And my niece and god-daughter, Gabriella,
    sits beside me; her communion was yesterday Ashling,
    so this is the afters! Like feckin weddings these. And it's
my mum's last Sunday roast –
    Saoi síos, sit down, she says.

And Gabby is up on her chair.

Gabby stands up on her chair.

Gabriella Before we eat,

Saoirse She says –

Gabriella I am not seen in church the way the boys are, which means I am not seen in my country the way the boys are which means I am not seen in this man-made world, so how do I know I am seen in heaven?

Saoirse I fucking love this child.

and she takes out her communion note book –

Gabriella This is what I wrote after the compassion for the dresses.

Saoirse She says. We learnt the word yesterday – I says. Yeno when Tom Brady wanted to wear her communion dress. And she wanted to wear the priest's dress. And nobody got to wear what they wanted. So, we had compassion for everyone!

Are you the next Oscalina Wildina? I says.

And she says –

Gabriella Ye need compassion at communions cuz Tom made more money off his and that's not fair,

most of the boys made more money than the girls,

like a trick the church is playing on us –

was it in the rule book for communions cuz

I didn't know I was going to make less money for being a girl.

So I have compassion for myself.

And Mum's jaw has hit the floor –

Brenda Jesus tonight that's a brilliant way of putting it –

Saoirse She says.

Brenda I've never made as much as your Granddad and I do all the work around here –

Saoirse And Gabby is back up on her chair.

Gabriella I want to be the same like the egg and spoon race.

Ye start on the same line, and I usually beat Tom in that one –

Cuz no one holds me back!

Saoirse She says.

Saoirse looks out through the window. She sees the robin sitting still; in the centre of the blossoms.

And I look round the table, Gran in the centre.

Our last roast before they jet off –

And Gabriella our own angel child.

And Daisy's lost her head –

Daisy Saoirse stop telling everyone she's an angel –

the teachers been writing home thinking –

she's off her feckin head!

Saoirse And we spend the evening in the garden.

Saoirse watches the robin take flight in the mystical, evening light. After five seconds; darkness.

In darkness: sound of a flight landing.

Pilot Two exits are lit.

A door opens. Bright light burns, lowly.

Choose

Go cúramach.

Carefully.

Bright light begins to fade.

In this moment.

Saoirse Anois.

End of Play.

Note: Mother Earth restores, heals, reminds, renews;
   Hear her in the winds and rain,
   See her in the trees at dawn or in the evening, when
light is sparkly and bright.
   Taste her in a fruit never before tried.
   Embrace her beauty in all its imperfections; she is
perfect.
   As She is. As We are.
   Embody her in the spirit of life.
   Of living.
   Of Home . . .

SHOWER

This short film is dedicated to
all bereaved during the Covid pandemic
and to all the healthcare workers too.

With love and thanks to Denise.

This short film is dedicated to
all bereaved during the Covid pandemic
and to all the healthcare workers too.

With love and thanks to Denise.

Shower was first screened as part of the Abbey Theatre's *Dear Ireland* season on 28 April 2021. Aoife was played by Denise Gough.

Characters

Aoife

Shower. Early morning.

Aoife has just come back from a shift in ICU. She is a nurse.

Aoife Yeah it's dripping. Split-second intervals.

Light brown.

Not quite brown bread brown, half wholemeal.

Constant drip now like a long *ssss*. I've bandaged it with tape round the.

Whaddya call it yeno that thing.

The pole, tube.

You know the long stick thing.

The PIPE, yes the pipe. It's not my apartment.

How much will it cost?

–

Right, how soon can you get here?

–

I start shift then, can you come any earlier?

–

I'll leave a key under the mat.

Thank you.

You have a very Irish name for an Englishman. We have a whole brand of tea in your name, Barry!

I'd murder a cup.

–

It's exhausting.
    People can't be with their loved ones at the end yeno.

Very hard.
    Just now an elderly lady. I held her hand

–

It's my job, like you plumbin we're all just doing our jobs!

–

Not easy, no Barry you're right!

Not as easy as this water is finding its way out its hole –
more of a dark brown bread colour now.

Like a pooish colour sorry I've a three-year-old we talk
about poo a lot.

–

Yeah.
    I haven't seen them in weeks.

We've a fifteen-year-old too who is very angry at her mum,
which is joyful.

I'd do anything for a long shower, they help me wash the
day away.

You couldn't pop up in the next hour?

–

I understand.

I've put a whaddya call it a, what are they called.

A bucket! Underneath.

If it keeps going I reckon I could bathe in it!

I'd probably be able to sit in it.

We jumped off the Forty Foot at Christmas.

I'd love to jump in there right now.

–

Well I thought about going back to Ireland to help but England's raised me too so I feel conflicted.

And a bit of shame around that, actually.
    My heart is in Ireland but my feet are in England. I got to be where my feet are.

I'm staying *here*. I love Ireland my heart will always be there but, we've stopped Barry the drip has come to a halt is that good or bad?

–

What would we do without you, Barry you're a hero.

Well, just being on the phone is nice. My friend left your number on the side.

BARRY THE PLUMBER!

Here's one for ye, what country eats the most cornflakes in the world?

–

Give it a guess. No, Ireland!

–

Yeah.
    Hang on hang on text from my daughter:

'Dad's made shitty salty ribs for the sixth night in a row. I've become a vegetarian.'

She's at that age.
    She doesn't like me being away.

No no, yeah she's high risk it's a yeah, a.
Mm Mm Mm.
Eh.
Mm.
–

A shower would be perfect.
My skin feels like it might fall off you know those feckin

suits they have us in I reckon I'm losing ten pounds a day
just the heat of them alone, running round.

And a tea, but I've no running water and a leaky pipe!
　　Blinding headache too, the goggles.
　　Oh, Ciara, hang on:

'Mum you didn't buy cornflakes.'

That's great isn't it Barry? Just what you want to hear. She's
calling. Stay there.

–

Hello Ciara,

–

I know I know baby why don't you watch a movie.
　　Yeah, a nice one.

–

Could you say a prayer?
　　No sorry sorry sorry Jesus, okay –
　　Are you wearing a coat?

–

Good girl, I know.

–

You're doing brilliantly.

–

Not long I promise.

–

Yes we can Skype I'm just onto the plumber darling and
I've work again in a few hours.
I'll Skype you as soon as I can okay?
Love you too.

Okay. Bye bye.

   Aoife puts her earpiece back in.

Barry you still there?

Thank God, we've stopped dripping but the pipe is
pulsating.

–

She's grand. Do you've kids?
   Spoke too soon we're dripping again we're back to the
drip.

More of a clear colour looks, drinkable.

–

No no I won't, it just looks refreshing.

It has its own little heartbeat, pulsing pipes!

Oh Barr-rrrry Boy, the pipes the pipes are calling – come fix
my pipes or I'll jump out the windowwww, I want a hug
but nobody will touuucccchh me –

I'm delirious, can you tell?

–

The lady who passed today, Gale, lovely dear sweet Gale –
she had an underlying heart condition. Made me think of
Ciara.

Don't know when I'll see her next.

Her family FaceTimed.

Gale's.

I found her iPad and they said their goodbyes. That's rare, usually there's not enough time.

Hold my mum's hand, that's what her daughter kept saying to me.

'Please please please just hold my mum's hand. Hold her.'

I held her.
    I didn't let go till a long while after.

–

I'm just doing my job –
    We're dripping again.

    Aoife checks her phone again. She reads out another text.

'Mum I'm watching an eighteens movie, Dad said I could, what's the Netflix password?'

Whaddya reckon Barry do I give her the password?

Good idea.

    Aoife texts aloud as she types.

Ask, your, father.

She doesn't usually speak to me this much, it's like we're all coming out of isolation *in* isolation.

I'm honoured. Spoke too soon!

    Aoife reads another text.

'You ruin my life.'

The bitch.
    Sorry.
    I didn't mean that.

–

THESE GODDAMN PIPES!

–

Uh thanks you're very good.

–

Thanks for staying on the phone.
    Thanks for listening. You're very good.

–

Yeah I'll get some sleep.

–

Think I have a pasta pot.

–

Oh nonono honestly I'm grand for food.

–

Are you sure? Number forty-eight. Thank you.

   Aoife turns the tap on. The water flows freely.
We're suckin diesal Barry!

–

   Aoife breaks down.